AF598742

DAD,
I made you a
BOOK

DEAR **DAD**,

I made this book for you because you're a great dad. Thank you for ALL that you do and ALL the ways you help me grow. I've included some of them here in these pages, but there are just TOO MANY to fit into one book. I made this ESPECIALLY for you because you really are ONE OF A KIND.

Love,

HERE'S ME!

DAD, YOU MAKE OUR FAMILY A

family.

WE LOVE EACH OTHER A LOT!

HERE, I DREW A PICTURE OF
us together.

I KNOW THAT
YOU ARE ALWAYS,
ALWAYS
HAPPY TO SEE ME.

I made this smiley face because

I'm happy when I see you too.

I can tell
YOU WORK HARD
to take care of
our family.

Thank you for doing things like

____

and ______________________________.

I really look up
to you, you know.
When I grow up,
I hope I am as
as you are.

HERE'S a PICTURE OF ME
ALL GROWN UP!

Thanks to you,
I'm very SMART.

If you asked me,
I could count
as high as
this number:

That's how many

I'd like to give you.

You and I are a lot **ALIKE.**

Like how we both ______________.

But we're also **DIFFERENT!**

Like how you like ______________

and I like ______________.

And together,
you and I are
BOREDOM
BUSTERS!
I love it so much when we

I just had to draw
a picture of it:

Sometimes I wonder if you can do

ANYTHING.

I imagine you could:

(check the boxes)

☐ INVENT A NEW KIND OF DANCE
☐ PLANT A TREE THAT GROWS ICE CREAM CONES
☐ JUGGLE ONE HUNDRED WATER BALLOONS

YOU SUPPORT ME IN SO MANY WAYS, BUT IT'S NOT *JUST* ME!

I've made a list of more people you help:

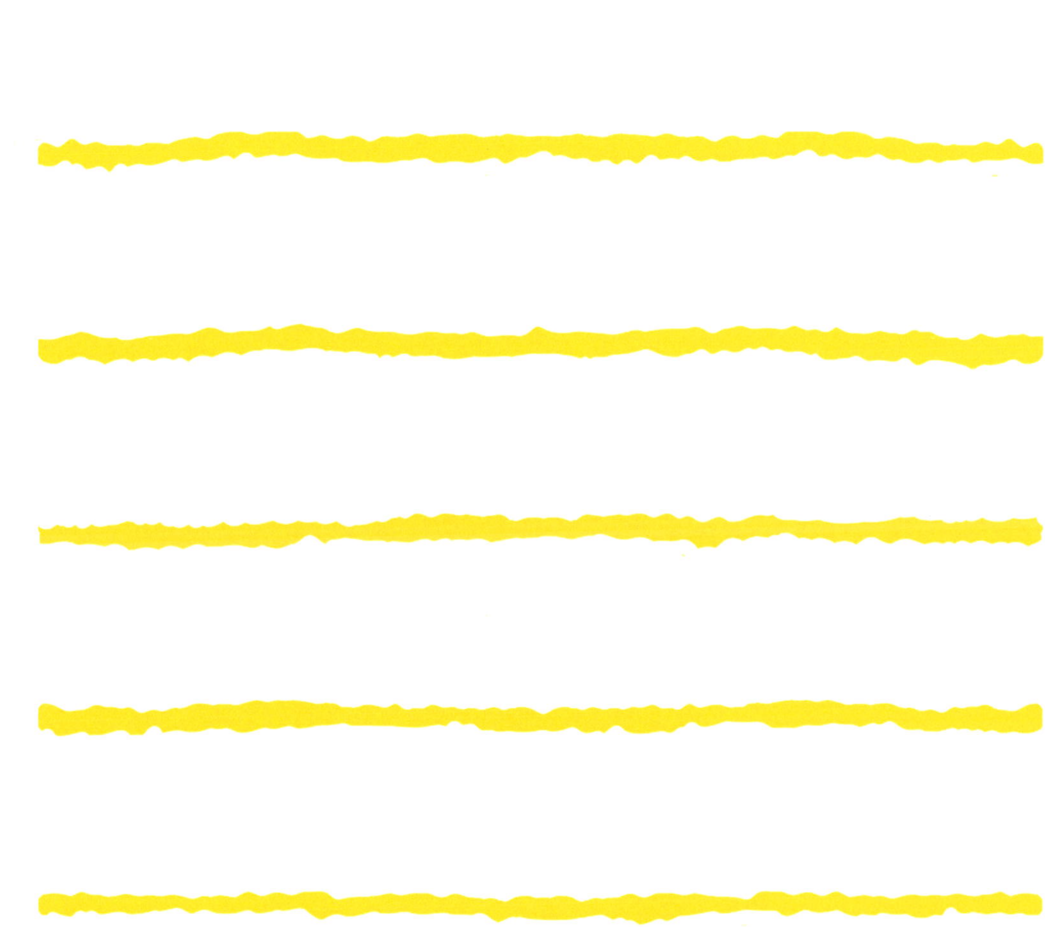

So, here's a
BIG THANK-YOU
HIGH FIVE
for being so awesome.

(TRACE HAND)

You deserve a gazillion MORE!

CELEBRATIONS WITH YOU
ARE ALWAYS FUN.

You probably know that my favorite holiday is

______________________.

That's when we

____

together.

(I LOVE THAT ABOUT US.)

REMEMBER THAT TIME WE ____________________

____

____________________________?

THAT'S ONE OF MY FAVORITE MEMORIES.

I LIKE TO DREAM
THAT ONE DAY
YOU AND I WILL

____

____.

HERE, LET ME GIVE YOU THIS AWARD.

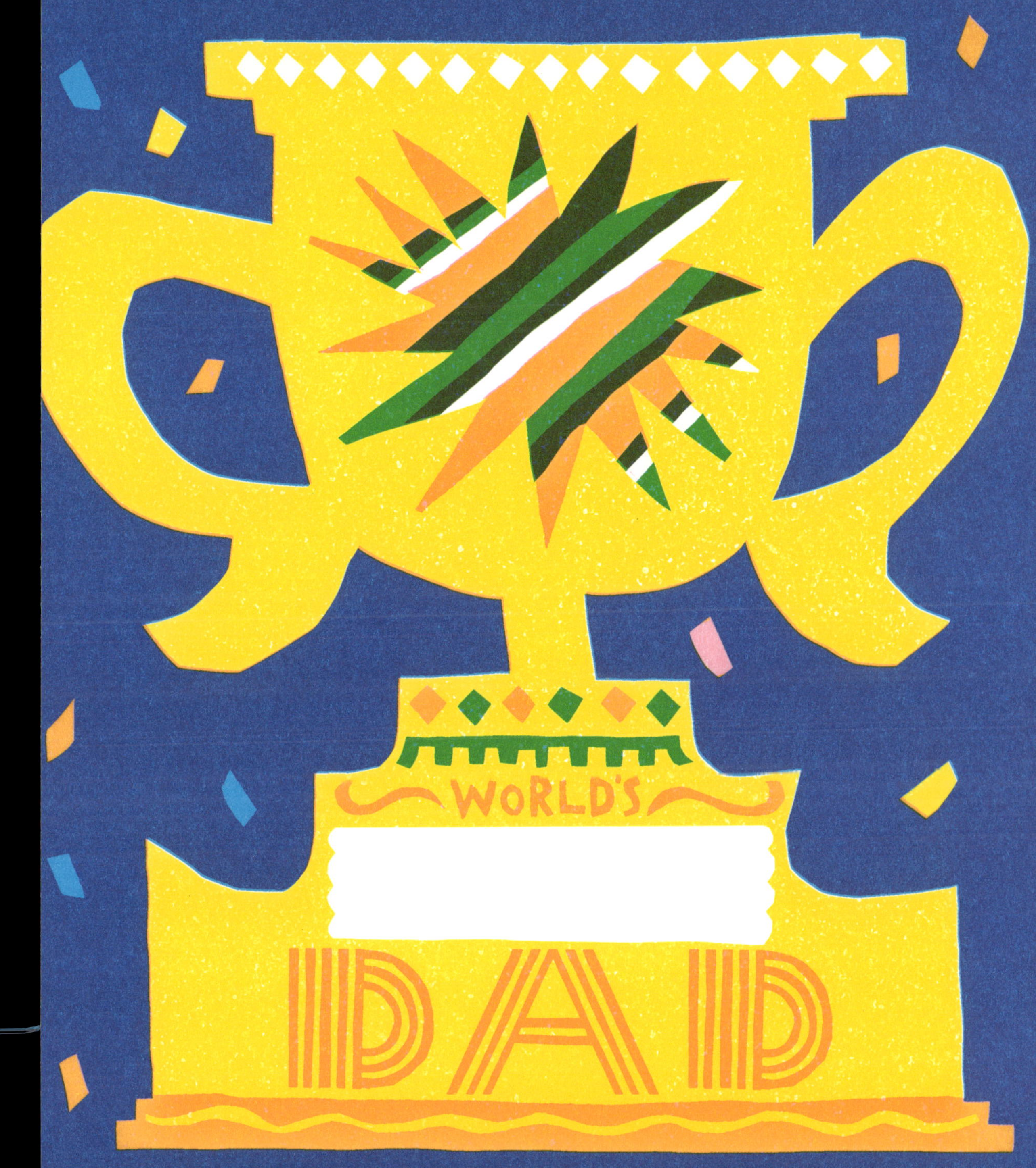
WORLD'S
DAD

Thank you, Dad. Because of you, I Know that:

(check the boxes)

- ☐ You are always there for me
- ☐ We'll have lots more ADVENTURES
- ☐ I AM LOVED
- ☐ You help me be ME
- ☐

(WRITE YOUR OWN!)

BECAUSE OF YOU,
WE ARE A
FAMILY.

Written by: Miriam Hathaway
Illustrated by: Asahi Nagata
Edited by: Bailey Vega
Art Directed by: Justine Edge

ISBN: 978-1-957891-47-7

1st printing. Printed in China with soy inks on FSC®-Mix certified paper. A012409001

Create meaningful moments with gifts that inspire.

CONNECT WITH US

live-inspired.com | sayhello@compendiuminc.com

@compendiumliveinspired
#compendiumliveinspired